BUILDING JEWISH LIFE

Rosh Ha-Shanah & Yom Kippur

by Joel Lurie Grishaver

photographs by Jane Golub, Joel Lurie Grishaver
and Alan Rowe
additional photography by Bill Aron

illustrated by Joel Lurie Grishaver
additional line art by Linda Nusbaum

with an original midrash by Rabbi Marc Gellman

Torah Aura Productions
Los Angeles, California

For Evelyn Borovsky-Roskin.
A voice which swept the King's chamber with joy.

Thank You:
Temple Beth El, San Pedro
Temple B'nai Israel, Sacramento
Temple Emanuel, Beverly Hills
Temple Beth Israel, Houston
Shir Chadash, Encino
Shirley Barish
Janice Alper
Judy Aronson
Andrea Kipnis
Merrill, Sarra & Alana Alpert
Harriet & Steven Rein

Our Advisory Committee:
Melanie Berman, Sherry Bissel-Blumberg, Gail Dorph,
Paul Flexner, Carolyn Starman-Hessel, Freda Huberman,
Cantor Jeffrey Klepper, Rabbi Lawrence Kushner,
Debi Mahrer, Fran Pearlman, Peninnah Schram

Our contributors
photographs on pages 7 and 10 © Bill Aron
The Announcing Tool, reprinted with permission of the
author, Rabbi Marc Gellman
illustrations for *Did Elana Do T'shuvah?* © Linda Nusbaum

Our Professional Services:
copyeditor: Carolyn Moore-Mooso
Alef Type & Design
Alan's Custom Lab
Gibbons Color Lab
Delta Lithograph

Library of Congress Cataloging-in-Publication Data
Grishaver, Joel Lurie.
  Building Jewish Life — Rosh Ha-Shanah & Yom Kippur

  Summary: Explores the history, significance, and
customs of Rosh Ha-Shanah and Yom Kippur and how
the holidays are celebrated in the synagogue. Includes
prayers from the Mahzor and discussion questions.
  1. High Holidays — Juvenile literature.   2. Rosh
Ha-Shanah — Juvenile literature.   3. Yom
Kippur — Juvenile literature.   4. High Holidays —
Liturgy —Texts — Juvenile literature.   5. Judaism —
Liturgy — Texts — Juvenile literature. [1. High Holidays.
2. Rosh Ha-Shanah.   3. Yom Kippur.   4. Fasts and
feasts — Judaism]   I. Golub, Jane Ellen, ill.   II. Rowe,
Alan Brahm, ill.   III. Title.
BM693.H5G75   1987   296.4'31   87-13949
          ISBN 0-933873-17-4 $4.95

Torah Aura Productions
4423 Fruitland Avenue
Los Angeles, California 90058

Manufactured in the United States of America.

ROSH HA-SHANAH

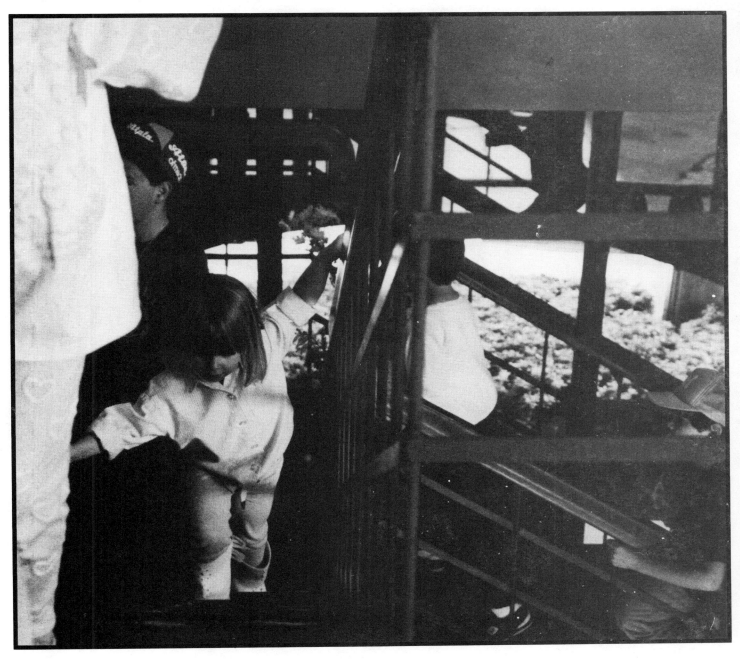

Think about the first day of school.

Everything is new. Everyone is dressed in new clothes and every backpack or school bag is filled with new pencils, rulers, erasers and other school supplies. Every notebook is filled with new paper. On the first day of school, you go to a new class with a new teacher and start a new year of learning.

The first day of
school is both
exciting and scary.

It is a day when
you worry about
lots of questions:

"Will this be
     a good year?"

"Will it be
     like last year?"

"Will I have
     lots of friends?"

"Will I make
     new friends?"

"Will my teacher
     like me?"

"Will I do well?"

The first day of
school is also a day
for making wishes:

"I hope that I have
     a good year."

"I hope that
everyone likes me."

"I hope I can be a
     good student."

"I hope that school
will be a lot of fun."

The feeling of being both excited and scared at the same time is called **awe**.[1] People feel **awe** when they meet someone very important or famous. They feel **awe** when they look at the Grand Canyon or a beautiful sunset, and they feel **awe** when they start something new. Often, something which is very exciting can also be scary.

Footnotes are found on pages 92-93.

The start of a school year is a new beginning. Everything which happened last year has been left behind. We go to a new class, with a new teacher who will open a new grade book. We have a fresh start. Our new teacher doesn't know us, doesn't know about the stupid mistakes we made and doesn't even know about the wonderful work we have done. We must start again.

Rosh Ha-Shanah means "Head of the Year." It is a Jewish holiday which comes in the fall, just about the same time as the start of school. It, too, is a day for asking questions and making wishes.

Rosh Ha-Shanah is a Jewish way of beginning the year with a fresh start. It gives us a chance to leave last year behind, and again try to be the best people we can become. Rosh Ha-Shanah begins the **Days of Awe**.[2]

Rosh Ha-Shanah is a time when we send cards to our friends and family. We send the wish *L'shanah Tovah*—for a good year. The start of a new year is a time for making wishes. Every Rosh Ha-Shanah card is a hope for the best possible new year.

Bill Aron

On Rosh Ha-Shanah we eat apples and honey. We also take the big, special, round Rosh Ha-Shanah *ḥallah*[3] and dip it in honey. This is another way of wishing that the new year will be sweet and good.

Some holidays are days set aside for just having fun. On some holidays we have parties. On others we watch fireworks. And, on some holidays we give presents. Rosh Ha-Shanah is a very different kind of holiday.

Rosh Ha-Shanah is called **The Birthday of the Universe**,[4] but it isn't a day for parties. Rosh Ha-Shanah is a time we set aside for thinking, praying and being awakened by the call of the shofar.

This is a *shofar.*[5] It is a musical instrument made from a ram's horn. It makes a loud, sharp, shrieking sound. It is the kind of sound that cuts and bites, the kind of sound that makes you pay attention. On Rosh Ha-Shanah it is a mitzvah to listen to the shofar. The voice of the shofar teaches us how to begin the new year.

A ram's horn is hollow. To turn it into a shofar, it must be boiled, bent and cleaned. Finally, a mouthpiece is drilled and carved.

On Rosh Ha-Shanah the shofar is sounded 100 times. Its sound awakens us to the message of Rosh Ha-Shanah.

Bill Aron

The shofar makes three different sounds:

   Tekiah[6] is one long loud blast. It sounds like a person shouting.
   Shevarim[6] is three short blasts. It sounds like a person groaning.
   Teru'ah[6] is nine quick blasts. It sounds like a person crying.

The sound of the shofar is the sound of Rosh Ha-Shanah.

When we are asleep, the sound of the alarm clock is a warning that our wake-up time has come.

In ancient Israel, there were no sirens, no radios, and no public address systems. People used the shofar. The shofar was an announcing tool. It was the signal used to announce the beginning of a holiday. It was the way people were called together. And, it was used as a danger signal.

Sometimes we can be asleep even when we are awake. We can walk around like dreamers, and not really know everything we are doing. Sometimes we make mistakes because we are not paying enough attention.

On Rosh Ha-Shanah, the shofar is our warning signal. It asks us to become fully awake. It calls on each of us to pay total attention to starting the new year as the best person we can become.

Maimonides[7] was a famous Jewish teacher. When he listened to the shofar blasts, he thought he could almost hear a voice. When he heard the shofar, it seemed to say:

Wake up from your sleep. You are asleep.
Get up from your slumber. You are in a deep sleep.
Search your behavior. Become the best person you can.
Remember God, the One who created you.

Laws of Repentance, 3.4

Isaac Arama[8] was another famous Jewish teacher. When he listened to the blasts of the shofar, he heard something different in each of the three sounds.

When he heard the one long loud blast of the *Tekiah*, it sounded like a person shouting and cheering. It said to him, "You are lucky. You live in the wonderful world which God created."

When he heard the nine quick blasts of the *Teru'ah*, it sounded like a person crying. It felt sad and a little scary. It said to him, "You are not as good a person as you could be. This past year you have done many wrong things."

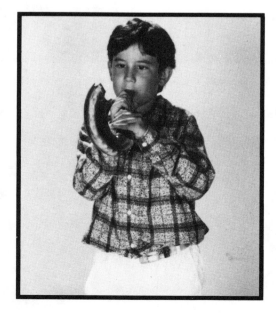

When he heard the three short blasts of the *Shevarim*, it sounded like a person groaning. It hurt a little bit. It said to him, "You have much work to do in order to become the best person you could be. You must start today."

The last of the 100 shofar blasts heard on Rosh Ha-Shanah is a *Tekiah Gedolah*. This is a "super" *Tekiah* where the person blowing the shofar makes the longest and loudest sound possible. It sounds like a big long loud cheer.

When Isaac Arama heard the *Tekiah Gedolah* it seemed to say to him,"I am proud of you. You've worked hard this Rosh Ha-Shanah. You are a good person. Next year you'll be even better."

On some holidays, the most important part of the celebration takes place at home. On Passover we have a Seder. On Thanksgiving we have a turkey dinner. And, on Ḥanukkah we light the Ḥanukkah Menorah and give gifts.

On Rosh Ha-Shanah families have special holiday meals, but the most important part of the celebration takes place in the synagogue. In the synagogue we use a special prayer book called a *Maḥzor.*[9]

On the following pages you will find a children's Mahzor. It can be used either as a text for worship, or as a way of preparing your child for a meaningful High Holy Day experience. The stories found within the service are perfect read-aloud material. The introduction to Yom Kippur continues on page 40.

YOM KIPPUR

ATONEMENT

Look at the word ATONEMENT.[10] Can you see two words hiding in it? Look carefully and you will find the words AT and ONE.

Ten days after Rosh Ha-Shanah comes the most serious and important day in the Jewish year. It is a day when Jews eat no food and spend all day praying. It is the day when we use all of our strength to return to being the best people we can be. It is a day when we try to again be *at one* with God. The day is sometimes called *shabbat ha-shabbaton*, the "super-shabbat." It is also called *Yom Kippur*, the day of AT-ONE-MENT.

This is a bathtub. It is a place were we wash off dirt and become clean again. Everyone needs a bath or a shower. No matter how careful you are, no matter how hard you try, you always get dirty. Everyone does. Being dirty is something you can always change. All you need is a little soap and water. Even when we are totally dirty, the bathtub can help us return to being clean.

Yom Kippur is a day when we try to become clean in a different way. It is the way Jews wash away all the mistakes and bad things they have done in the past year, and return to being the kind of people God wants. Yom Kippur is the way we return to being AT ONE with God.

These are a bow and arrows. The rabbis used a bow and arrow as a way of explaining *Yom Kippur*. Imagine you could pick up the bow and shoot at a target. You could pick up the bow, pull back the string and then send the arrow flying towards the target. Even if you were the best archer in the whole world, even if you were always very careful, sometimes you wouldn't hit the bull's-eye. Every once in a while, your arrow would *miss the mark* [11].

Trying to be a good Jew is a lot like being an archer.

We want to be kind. We want to help other people. We want to respect our parents and teachers. We want to control our tempers. We never want to hurt anyone. Being a good Jew is trying to be the best person you can be and trying to make the world the best possible place for everyone.

Even when we try with all of our might, we sometimes *miss the mark*. Sometimes we get excited. Sometimes we get angry. Sometimes we want to do something so much that even knowing that it is wrong doesn't stop us from doing it.

In an archery contest, no one would ever let you walk up to the target and take back the arrows which missed the bull's-eye. But, on *Yom Kippur* God allows us to take back the things we have done which *missed the mark.*

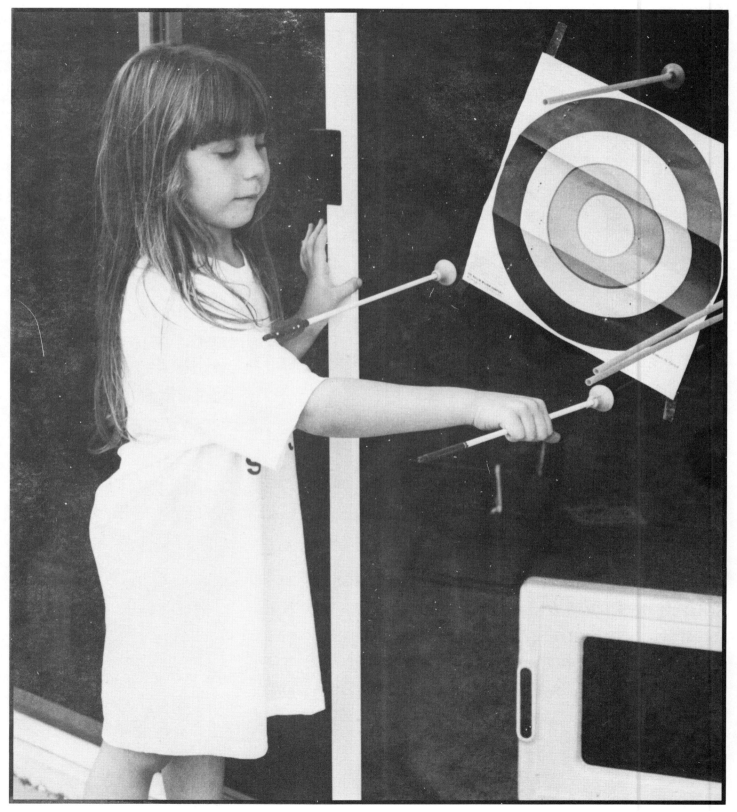

In a bathtub we wash away the dirt with soap, shampoo, brushes, washcloths and water. On *Yom Kippur* we use thoughts and songs to make our hearts clean again. On *Yom Kippur* we spend a whole day doing *t'shuvah.*

T'shuvah[12] is a Hebrew word which means "**coming back.**" *T'shuvah* is when we walk up to the target, take out all of the wrong things we have done which *missed the mark* and then **come back** to try again.

23

T'shuvah isn't just saying, "I am sorry." It is more than that. *T'shuvah* is doing everything we can to make sure that we never make the same mistake again. *T'shuvah* is hard work. It is feeling sorry with your whole heart. It is wanting with all your heart and strength to be the best person you can.

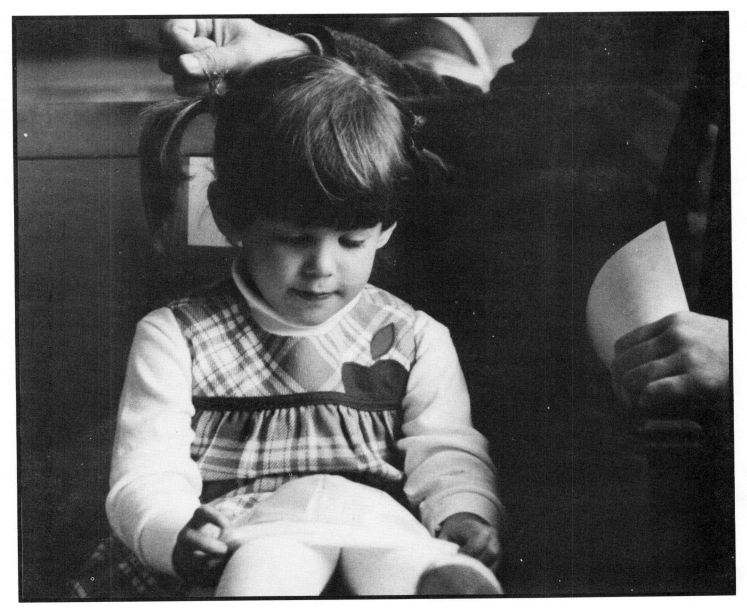

The rabbis taught that people can *miss the mark* in two different ways.

People can *miss the mark* by hurting other people and people can *miss the mark* by not being the kind of people God wants them to be.

Yom Kippur is a way of making peace with God. If we really do *t'shuvah* on this special day, God will forgive us. But, there is no special day for making peace with other people. There are no special prayers which let you do *t'shuvah* and take back something which hurt another human being. Each person must do this alone. To be a good Jew, a person must ask anyone he or she has hurt for forgiveness.

Did you ever do something really wrong and get caught? Remember....

You got yelled at and sent to your room. You were crying. You were both angry and sad. You were crying because you didn't like being yelled at and punished. You were crying because it hurt you to make your mother and father angry. You stayed in your room a long time. You didn't want to see your parents. You didn't want to get yelled at again, and you didn't want to have them look at you and remember the bad thing you had done. You just wanted to be alone.

After a long time, you stopped crying. You were not so angry any more, and you didn't want to keep feeling sad. So, you came out of your room and walked very carefully towards your mother or father. Maybe you hid behind a door so that you could make sure that it was all right. Then, after a little while you found the strength to say, "I'm really sorry. I promise that I will never ever do that again." After a long pause, arms opened, and you ran and got a big hug. You were told, "I know you really mean that. I forgive you and I love you very much." Once again you were **one** family.

Yom Kippur is the day when God allows us to feel truly sorry and come back to being AT ONE. That is the meaning of ATONEMENT.

By fasting and spending a whole day in prayer, we use all our strength to take back the things we have done which *missed the mark.* We try to do *t'shuvah* with all our heart. The words in the *mahzor* explain our hopes that on Yom Kippur we can ATONE and return to being AT ONE with God.

ACTIVITIES

SUNDAY	MONDAY	TUESDAY	WEDNESDAY	THURSDAY	FRIDAY	SATURDAY
September Elul/Tishre			1 27 Elul	2 28 Elul	3 Erev Rosh Ha-Shanah 29 Elul	4 Rosh Ha-Shanah First Day 1 Tishre
5 Rosh Ha-Shanah Second Day 2 Tishre	6 Fast of Gedaliah 3 Tishre	7 4 Tishre	8 5 Tishre	9 6 Tishre	10 Erev Shabbat 7 Tishre	11 Shabbat Shuvah 8 Tishre
12 Erev Yom Kippur Kol Nidre 9 Tishre	13 Yom Kippur 10 Tishre	14 11 Tishre	15 12 Tishre	16 13 Tishre	17 Erev Sukkot 14 Tishre	18 First Day of Sukkot 15 Tishre
19 Second Day of Sukkot 16 Tishre	20 17 Tishre	21 18 Tishre	22 19 Tishre	23 20 Tishre	24 Hoshanah Rabbah 21 Tishre	25 Shemini Atzeret 22 Tishre
26 Simhat Torah 23 Tishre	27 24 Tishre	28 25 Tishre	29 26 Tishre	30 27 Tishre		

This is a Jewish Calendar for the month of September. It shows both the dates of the Gregorian Calendar and the dates of the Jewish year. *Use this calendar to help you answer these questions.*

1. The Hebrew month which comes before *Rosh Ha-Shanah* is called _____ During this month Jews get ready for *Rosh Ha-Shanah* and *Yom Kippur.*

2. *Rosh Ha-Shanah* comes on the first and second days of the Hebrew month of _____ .

3. *Yom Kippur* comes on the ____ day of this month.

4. The ten days from *Rosh Ha-Shanah* to *Yom Kippur* are called _____ .

Days of Awe

T'shuvah

Tishre

Elul

Tenth

29

Jews prepare for Rosh Ha-Shanah in many different ways:

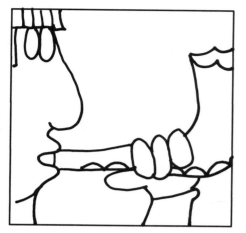
Practicing blowing the shofar

Giving Tzedakah

Sending Rosh Ha-Shanah cards

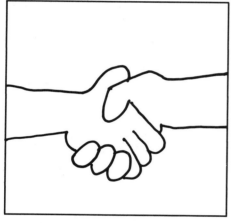
Saying "I'm sorry"

Studying the Mahzor

Remembering family history

Discuss these customs. Explain why each one is a good way of getting ready for the Days of Awe. Both parent and child should pick the one custom which each of them think would best help them get ready to celebrate Rosh Ha-Shanah and Yom Kippur and explain why. Parents should write down their answers and their child's answers.

CHILD

_____'s way of getting ready is _____ .

This will help me get ready for the Days of Awe by _____

_____ .

PARENT

_____'s way of getting ready is _____ .

This will help me get ready for the Days of Awe by _____

_____ .

There are 4 different kinds of shofar blasts:

Tekiah ▬▬▬▬▬▬ (1 long blast)
Shevarim ▬▬ ▬▬ ▬▬ (3 short blasts)
Teru'ah ▪▪▪▪▪▪▪▪▪ (9 quick blasts)
Tekiah Gedolah ▬▬▬▬▬▬▬▬ (a very long blast)

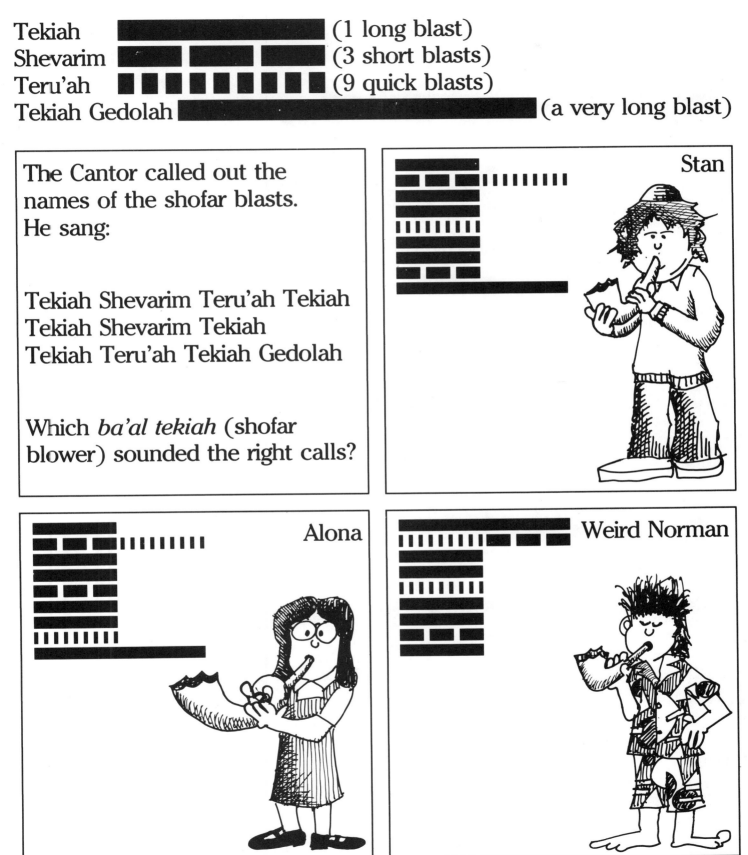

The Cantor called out the names of the shofar blasts. He sang:

Tekiah Shevarim Teru'ah Tekiah
Tekiah Shevarim Tekiah
Tekiah Teru'ah Tekiah Gedolah

Which *ba'al tekiah* (shofar blower) sounded the right calls?

Stan

Alona

Weird Norman

31

THE STORY OF A SHOFAR

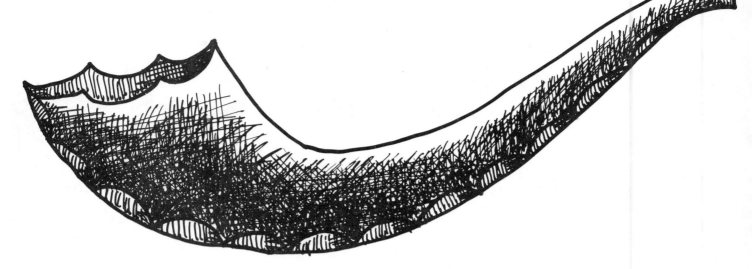

Read and complete this story together. Parents should write down their child's answers.

I am a shofar. I belong to Mr. Melvin Berman. I make the sounds which awaken people's hearts to the message of Rosh Ha-Shanah.

When Jews hear me calling, they_____

_____.

I was made from the _____.
It took a lot of work to make me. I had to be boiled and scraped, shaped, and even drilled.

It also takes a lot of work to learn how to sound my calls. I was bought for Mel when he was ten years old. He tried hard to learn how to make a good *tekiah*, a good _____, a good _____, and a great, long _____ *gedolah*.

It takes a lot of practice to be a great *Ba'al Tekiah*. When Mel first put me to his lips, it sounded sick. It sounded like a _____

_____.

Today, Mel is the best shofar blower in the whole synagogue. He teaches others how to shape the right sounds. On Rosh Ha-Shanah, he can sound a *tekiah gedolah* which seems to last _____

_____.

Jews know that trying to be the best person you can be is a lot like trying to be a great archer. Even when we try our hardest, we sometimes *miss the mark*. On *Rosh Ha-Shanah* and *Yom Kippur* we look back on the past year and see how close to a bull's-eye our life has been.

Circle the correct answers:

1. In the past year, I have *missed the mark* by using words carelessly.

   Not at all   A little   Some   A lot

2. In the past year, I have *missed the mark* by being sneaky.

   Not at all   A little   Some   A lot

3. In the past year, I have *missed the mark* by lying.

   Not at all   A little   Some   A lot

4. In the past year, I have *missed the mark* by not respecting parents and teachers.

   Not at all   A little   Some   A lot

5. In the past year, I have *missed the mark* by being selfish.

   Not at all   A little   Some   A lot

6. In the past year, I have *missed the mark* by being too proud.

   Not at all   A little   Some   A lot

7. In the past year, I have *missed the mark* by not stopping myself from doing some things that I really wanted to do, even when I knew that they were wrong.

   Not at all   A little   Some   A lot

In the next year, the one way I want most to grow is by working on not *missing the mark* by_____. (Fill in a number).

Did Elana Do T'shuvah?

1.

Elana Holtz did not come from a large family, but her house often seemed too small. There were only Mother and Father, Elana and her little brother Michael. Sometimes Elana thought that four was too many. There was also an old grey cat named Gluckle von Hamlin, but she wasn't part of the problem.

Elana liked cooking, reading, playing with her doll named Crystal, pretending to have a video on MTV, having Gluckle fall asleep in her lap, putting on her mother's clothes and makeup, and riding skateboards with Berta Cooper. Berta's real name was Roberta. Elana didn't like other people telling her what to do. Everyone else had their idea of what Elana was supposed to do.

It was one of those days. In school, Mr. Hoyt spent the whole day giving orders. It seemed that everything Elana did was wrong. She wanted to finish her reading book, but Mr. Hoyt said that it was math time. When she and Berta wanted to work in the science center, Mr. Hoyt said it was Baxter and David's turn. Elana wanted indoor recess, but Mr. Hoyt thought it was warm enough to go outside. Then, the art teacher was sick, so they had an extra period of spelling. And so it went. Elana came home from school in a bad mood.

She sat at the kitchen table having her snack. She thought about making a chocolate cake. She got out the bowl, the big spoon, the pan, the mix, the water, the eggs, the butter and everything. Then, Mother came home and told her to clean up the kitchen. Mother was going to fix dinner. There was no time for the chocolate cake. Elana was angry. She yelled at her mother, turned her back, and slammed the kitchen door.

Elana went into the family room and turned on the TV. She was dancing and singing to MTV. Her father came home. He came into the family room with his newspaper and sat in his big chair. From behind the newspaper he told her turn the television off and do her homework. Elana was angry. She yelled at her father and ran upstairs to her room. She played her radio as loud as it could go.

Michael came into her room. He didn't knock. He wanted her to play with him. She said, "No." He said, "Please..." Before he could even say another word, Elana yelled at him. He left her room. Elana picked up Gluckle and went into her closet. Together they sat in the dark on the floor.

On Rosh Ha-Shanah the services were very long. Elana sat there very quietly. She was almost crying. The rabbi told a story about a poor boy who had no parents and who was too poor to go to school. He had to work hard every day. When Rosh Ha-Shanah came, he didn't even know how to read the words in the prayer book. Elana said to herself, "I am very lucky." The boy in the story still prayed to God with all his heart. Elana said to herself, "I will too."

When the rabbi explained that *t'shuvah* meant "coming back" from doing bad things, Elana made up her mind. This Rosh Ha-Shanah was going to be her new beginning. She made a promise that from that day on, she  would never ever get angry and yell at her family. She was going to try with all her might to never *miss that mark* again.

That night after father finished the read-aloud time and after the lights were turned out, Elana stayed awake. She sat in the bed and thought about her promise. She remembered all the times she had gotten angry too fast. She remembered all the times she yelled with no good reason. Again, she promised with all her heart to make this year a new beginning. Gluckle jumped up on the bed and the two of them fell asleep.

It was Yom Kippur morning. Father came in to wake Elana. She wanted to sleep for five more minutes. He said, "There just isn't time." He pulled the blankets off the bed. Elana wanted to yell, but she remembered her promise and stopped.

She put on her good dress and went down stairs. She took a plastic cup from the top of the sink and filled it with orange juice. Michael came in and said, "You're not supposed to eat or drink—stupid." Elana had forgotten. She started to yell at Michael and then stopped herself. She threw the plastic cup full of orange juice into the sink. Some of it splashed on her dress. She walked out of the kitchen.

She met Mother in the hall. First Mother said, "Good morning, dear." Then she said, "There is something on your dress; you will have to change." Elana screamed, "I know," and ran into her room.

4.

At Yom Kippur services Elana began to cry. When they read the long list of things people do wrong called the *Al Ḥeyt*, Father noticed the tears. Michael thought it was funny, but Mother put her hand on his shoulder. Father took her out into the hall. She said, "I lied to God." Father didn't understand. She said, "On Rosh Ha-Shanah I promised that I would never get angry and yell at anyone ever again." Father understood. He said, "No one is perfect." Elana didn't understand.

Father said, "Real *t'shuvah* is very hard. Everyone misses the mark; that is why we have Rosh Ha-Shanah and Yom Kippur every year. These holidays help us to direct our hearts and try our best." Elana just said, "Real *t'shuvah* is very hard." Together, the two of them went back into the services. Elana whispered, "Mother, I'm sorry I yelled." Then she said in her heart, "Today, I am again going to make a new beginning—again."

Answer these questions:

1. Was Crystal the name of Elana's cat?   YES   NO

2. Did Elana's Father like MTV?   YES   NO

3. What promise did Elana make?_____

3. Did Elana really mean the promise she made to God on Rosh Ha-Shanah?   YES   NO

4. On Rosh Ha-Shanah and Yom Kippur, Jews work hard to make the new year a new beginning. We call this pointing of our heart towards being the best people we can be _____

5. Did Elana do real *t'shuvah?*   YES   NO

BUILDING JEWISH LIFE

A Partnership

This **Building Jewish Life** curriculum was designed in the belief that the best possible Jewish education happens only when the classroom and the home are linked. These pages are designed to cycle back and forth between those two realms, and to be used as a tool for learning in each. For this material to work most effectively, teacher and parent must assume interlocking roles and share in actualizing Jewish values and expressions. Each will do it in his/her own way. Each will do it with his/her own style. Together, they will reinforce each other, offering the child tangible experience and understanding of a visionary tradition.

Mitzvah Centered

Mitzvot is a word which means "commanded actions" and is used to describe a series of behaviors which Jewish tradition considers obligations. Classical Judaism teaches that the fabric of Jewish life is woven of 613 of these mandated actions. This series is built around the mitzvot, but it uses the term somewhat differently. In our day and age, the authority behind any "command" or obligation is a matter of personal faith and understanding. Each Jew makes his/her own peace or compromise with the tradition, affording it a place in his/her own life. In our age, the mitzvot have become rich opportunities. They are the things which Jews do, the activities by which we bring to life the ethics, insights, and wisdom of our Jewish heritage. Such acts as blessing holiday candles, visiting the sick, making a seder, comforting mourners, feeding the hungry, hearing the Purim megillah, studying Torah, educating our children, and fasting on Yom Kippur are all part of the mitzvah—Jewish behavior— "opportunity" list. They are actions which, when they engage us, create moments of celebration, insight, and significance. It is through the mitzvot that the richness of the Jewish experience makes itself available. Without addressing the "authority" behind the mitzvot, and without assuming "obligation," this series will expose the power of many mitzvah-actions and advocate their performance based on the benefit they can bring to your family. It does so comfortably, because we know that you will explore this material and make decisions which are meaningful for you and your family.

The Classroom

In the classroom, this volume serves as a textbook. It helps the teacher introduce important objects, practices, personalities and places in Jewish life. It serves as a resource for exploring Jewish values and engages the students in

"making meaning" from Jewish sources. The inclusion of both a parent's guide and a teacher's guide at the end of this volume was an intentional act. We felt it was important for parents to fully understand what was being taught in the classroom.

The Home

This material suggests three different levels of home involvement. On the simplest level, it contains a number of parent-child activities which demand your participation. They cannot be completed without your help. None of these are information-centered. The task of teaching names, pronunciations and facts has been left for the classroom. Rather, these are all moments of sharing values and insights or experimenting with the application of that which has been learned in class. They should be wonderful experiences and they call upon you to be a parent interested in his/her child, not a skilled teacher or tutor.

On a second level, much of this material can also be used to provide "read-aloud" experiences at bedtime, or as the basis for family study and discussion at the dinner table. Do not be afraid to "pre-empt" that which will be taught in class, or to "review" that which your child has learned. The more reinforcement, the better.

Finally, and most dramatically, there is the experience of participating in the mitzvot described in this book. We strongly urge you to make this a year to "try out" as many of them as possible. Think of them as the field trips and home experiments which will enrich the classroom experience and make it comprehensible.

The Network

The prime focus of this text series is celebration. Celebrations are better when they are shared with friends. New activities and new challenges are easier when they are shared. Familiar activities are also enriched by the presence of others. Many of the congregations which adopt this series will already have a system of Havurot, Jewish Holiday Workshops, or family activities. Others will organize parallel parent education sessions and special events for the families of the students in this program. We also imagine that some families will network with their friends to "try out" some of these mitzvah-events. It is our strong suggestion that, at least on an event-to-event basis, you connect with other Jewish families to experience some of the celebrations about which your child will be learning.

The High Holidays

Rosh Ha-Shanah and Yom Kippur center on reflections, not actions. In practice, they consist of long days spent in the synagogue. Perplexingly, the most important days in the Jewish year are not child-centered; and in fact, they are not experiences which easily invite children's participation. As educators and parents, we do our best to make Rosh Ha-Shanah into a celebration of apples and honey, to make Yom Kippur into the great ritual "I'm Sorry." We expose the parts of the observance which have the potential to speak directly to our young. We strive to structure their participation in a limited way in order to set the pattern for later development. However, in truth, the Days of Awe are R-rated adult experiences. R-rated for seriousness, maturity, and complexity.

There is, of course, an irony. In order to immerse ourselves in the sense of renewal and reconciliation offered by these Days of Awe, we need to be in touch with much of our childhood experience. As adults we expect perfection. When a person makes a commitment, he or she is expected to keep it. When we witness failure, we treat it with great cynicism. Children don't have that expectation. They understand that growing and changing take a long time. They know that being a year older doesn't make you a complete adult. Rosh Ha-Shanah and Yom Kippur are rooted in directing your heart and wishing with all your might. They are times to put away the cynicism of self-fulfilling prophecy, our knowledge about patterning, our insights into the psychology of human development—and to believe profoundly, with wide-eyed innocence, that this time we can do better.

"On Rosh Ha-Shanah all the inhabitants of the world pass before God in judgment like a flock of sheep."

Despite this complexity of image and practice, Rosh Ha-Shanah and Yom Kippur offer us two important interrelated insights to share with our children—insights which can help to shape the way they grow and develop.

The first lesson: No matter what has gone before, we can always make a new beginning. While we have to take the responsibility for what has already happened, we can always start again to make things better. That is the essence of Rosh Ha-Shanah.

The second lesson: A person is always responsible for what he/she does. When we make a mistake, when we miss the mark, we have to do more than feel sorry. We have to both do our best to correct the hurt we caused another person, and do our best to see to it that we never ever do the same thing again. This is t'shuvah (repentance), the action demanded by Yom Kippur.

Rosh Ha-Shanah

Origins

Imagine a world where the seasons didn't automatically cycle, where you weren't sure that the life-giving winter rains would indeed follow the long hot summer. Imagine a world where religious celebration actually

exercised a cause-and-effect influence on nature, and you can understand the origins of Rosh Ha-Shanah.

In ancient Babylon, they used to believe that the world went into limbo between one year and the next. In their reality, the start of the next year was directly dependent on the active decision of the gods. Between the years, Marduk and his gang would meet in a heavenly "room-of-fate" and decide the fate of humanity and the rest of creation. While this celestial annual meeting was taking place, the Babylonians celebrated their little hearts out, staging reenactments of the gods' greatest feats and doing everything possible to positively influence their verdict.

In the Mishnah, the formative description of Rosh Ha-Shanah is given. We are told,

> "On Rosh Ha-Shanah all the inhabitants of the world pass before God in judgment like a flock of sheep."
> (Rosh Ha-Shanah 1.2)

The Talmud expands this image of judgment, stating,

> "Three books are opened on Rosh Ha-Shanah. One is for the totally wicked. One is for the completely righteous. One is for everybody else. The righteous are instantly inscribed and sealed for life. The wicked are directly inscribed and fated to death. For those who are in between, judgment is suspended from Rosh Ha-Shanah to Yom Kippur. If they demonstrate merit, they too will be sealed for life..."(Rosh Ha-Shanah 13b)

The Jewish vision of annual renewal shares with the Babylonian a sense that human action makes a difference. It begins with the assumption that the way we approach the new year can effect the cosmic order. Rosh Ha-Shanah becomes unique in its spotlighting of the ethical. While the instinct to begin a new year with resolutions and new convictions even touches our Roman—influenced secular New Year's celebration, the mandating of a deep introspection and self-accounting by every individual is a uniquely Jewish commitment.

Two Opportunities

The Torah tells us very little about Rosh Ha-Shanah. We are simply told, "In the seventh month, on the first day of the month, you shall observe a holy day: you shall not work at your occupation. You shall observe it as a day when the horn is sounded." (Numbers 29.1) In addition, a special holiday gift-offering was sacrificed. The synagogue-centered Rosh Ha-Shanah celebrations we know are creations of the Talmudic era. A biblical Rosh Ha-Shanah consisted of only two *mitzvot*: (1) taking the day off and (2) hearing the shofar.

You shall not work at your occupation. When the Torah spoke of not working on Rosh Ha-Shanah, it wasn't an order intended to force an individual to choose between going to work or going to services. Rosh Ha-Shanah, like Shabbat and the holidays, was intended to be a time when the whole village and all the surrounding farms stopped their normal tasks and everyone came together. Not working made Jewish holidays a time of total community. Freed from a day of labor, everyone was involved. In our society, Rosh Ha-Shanah actualizes an ingathering of the exiles. It actualizes (with the exception of community-wide celebrations of Israel and political protests) the largest Jewish assemblies we experience. Yet, unique to our experience is the reality that the price we pay for this sense of community is a feeling of separation from the larger and total society. Joining together on Rosh Ha-Shanah means separating ourselves from the other people with whom we work or study.

Staying out of school on Rosh Ha-Shanah (and Yom Kippur) is often the first definitional act of Jewish identity a child will experience. It is a boundary issue which separates Jews involved with their heritage from the rest of the general population. In some settings it is an easy and automatic thing to do. In others, it mandates a public declaration and perhaps some serious makeup work. At the same time, the total impact of the synagogue experience (regardless of the amount of time spent squirming in chairs and counting the pages left) is a profound sense of belonging.

You shall observe it as a day when the horn is sounded. The Torah makes it clear that hearing the shofar is the major Rosh Ha-Shanah exper-ience. In the Talmud and subsequent codes, the rabbis clarify in great detail the proper procedures for blowing and hearing the shofar. We learn that a shofar must be made only out of a ram's horn, may be decorated with carvings but not painted, that it may be covered with gold but must have a natural mouthpiece, etc. The exact procedure for the number and nature of shofar calls has also been very carefully prescribed. However, as with many Jewish practices, we are carefully guided in our perfor-mance, while left to strug-

gle with our own understanding of its meaning.

The midrash is rich in explanations (pick any one you want). They include associations with the horns heard at a king's coronation, the shofrot heard at Mount Sinai when the Torah was given, the piercing voices of the prophets, and the ram offered up in Isaac's place. They suggest that the shofar call will announce the final judgment, the coming of universal freedom, and begin the messianic "end of days." In addition, they associate the feelings generated by hearing its call with an awakening, a sense of history and a sense of humility. In short, we can hear in it anything and everything which moves us.

The shofar is Rosh Ha-Shanah's most tangible symbol. While its sound reflects the abstraction of the holiday's call, the actual horn and its specific calls are concrete and

---

> "In the seventh month, on the first day of the month, you shall observe a holy day: you shall not work at your occupation. You shall observe it as a day when the horn is sounded."

---

masterable. At Congregation Beth El in San Pedro, California, Rabbi David Lieb invited all who owned shofrot to join in blowing the final *tekiah gedolah* (on Yom Kippur). The end result of the invitation was that by the third or fourth year of the practice, close to twenty percent of the congregation had purchased shofrot, and in most of those families parents and children practiced shofar blowing together. The month of *Elul*, the month which precedes Rosh Ha-Shanah, is traditionally a time when the shofar is blown at every weekday morning service. The month of shofar calls serves a dual function. It both begins the dramatic buildup to the Days of Awe and gives the shofar blower time to practice. The Beth El custom recreates that experience in a wonderfully contemporary manner, making the act of learning and practicing the shofar a tangible preparation for Rosh Ha-Shanah and Yom Kippur.

Other Preparations

The hearing of the shofar is but one of the preparations for the High Holidays which the tradition has evolved. There are others.

The Torah Covers, Ark Curtain, Reading Desk covers, etc. are all exchanged for white covers.

Families visit the cemetery and spend time reconnecting with their family history and traditions.

Specific attention is paid to the giving of *tzedakah*, the righteous act of using our wealth to help those in need. This is both an act of *t'shuvah* and a setting of next year's patterns.

Greeting cards are sent to friends and family. These cards are expressions of our wishes and hopes for the coming year, and for the future.

These traditional practices can serve as jumping-off points for your own preparation for Rosh Ha-Shanah. Shopping for new clothes echoes the preparation of the sanctuary. Time spent with the family photo album can be a wonderful way of sharing your own history and traditions. Even sitting down as a family to write and mail checks to key causes and organizations can help to set the stage. Something as simple as making, signing, addressing and sending New Year's cards can be a significant learning experience, especially when the focus is placed on the wishes and hopes rather than the mechanics. Be as creative as you want—for the more you build the participation and anticipation, the more meaning these awesome days will hold.

T'shuvah, Tefillah, and Tzedakah

The central motif for Rosh Ha-Shanah is that of a trial. We enter our day in celestial courts, knowing that we are guilty and prepared to throw ourselves on the divine court's mercy. We find the formula for divine clemency in one of Rosh Ha-Shanah's most somber prayers, the *Unetaneh Tokef*. There it says, "*T'shu-vah*[12], *Tefillah* (prayer), and *Tzedakah* annul the severity of the judgment." The deep introspection focused by the Days of Awe is designed to direct us towards these three Jewish acts.

T'shuvah means "return." It is more a process of growth than guilt. While our surrounding secular culture teaches us much about guilt and regret, it is not as strong on redirection. Here the Jewish tradition provides a unique resource for inner strength. T'shuvah is, in actuality, a sort of a "mid-course correction." It is the process of renewing your vision of who you should be becoming, and then shifting your actions and commitments in that direction. T'shuvah needs to be thought of as a skill, a trained and refined ability to take account of one's life and then act on what was learned from the reflection. It is a skill which, if mastered, can provide an individual with the resources for continual growth and maturation.

T'shuvah is as difficult to teach as it is to talk about. As with learning to ride a bicycle, prior instruction only does half the job. Ultimately, you have to discover your own ability to balance and readjust. It is the kind of process which is best learned through example and imitation. There is much we can do to help our children discover their own way of doing t'shuvah. We can make sure that they can discover t'shuvah at home as well as in school. It should be a word which is made part of family conversations. It should be an act which is part of family practice.

The tradition teaches that people can *miss the mark* in two ways. Some mistakes are made against God, others are errors which hurt other people. If you do t'shuvah, God will forgive your *missings of the mark*. However, people must individually forgive you on their own. Therefore, in this awesome season, it is common practice for Jews to apologize for things done wrong, and renew their friendships by asking and granting forgiveness. One of the best possible models of introduction, would be a conversation where a

parent (in anticipation of Rosh Ha-Shanah) reviewed the year with his/her child and asked the child's forgiveness for the one or two times the parent's temper was lost, or other *missings of the mark*.

Likewise, there is a custom observed on the first day of Rosh Ha-Shanah called *tashlikh*. During the afternoon, Jews walk to the river, the ocean, or other nearby bodies of water to empty their pockets, which have been previously filled with bread crumbs, into the water. It is a symbolic casting away of sins. Many congregations have now expanded *tashlikh* into a major event. We also know of several families who have evolved their own family *tashlikh* event specifically for their children. In one case, things which *missed the mark* are inscribed in squeeze frosting on pieces of bread which are then cast into the river. In another case, behaviors which are to be left behind are written in a water soluble ink, and then cast into the water to literally wash away. Both of these are ways of making this abstract custom a more concrete introduction to *t'shuvah*. It should be noted that writing on Rosh Ha-Shanah is a violation of the traditional prohibition against work. The materials for the ceremony held on Rosh Ha-Shanah can be prepared in advance.

May the dreams of our children, and the children of the world, come true in 5746.

DANIEL, SHIRA, STEVE AND FRIEDA HUBERMAN

Tefillah is the Hebrew word for prayer. It comes from a root which means "thought." In the context of this booklet, it is impossible to provide a substantive introduction to the process of Jewish worship. The services found in the *Mahzor* section do, however, provide a first-level introduction. Reading and discussing them together in preparation or in review of an experience at the synagogue would do much to open the process of prayer to your child. The questions found in *italics* are designed to give you wonderful things to talk about.

You will also find that the special children's/family services included in this booklet are filled with stories. These were made for bedtime read-aloud experiences. Use them as often as you like.

Tzedakah, which is usually mistranslated as "charity," is a mitzvah which is labeled with a root connected to the idea of "righteousness." The Jewish tradition sees the giving of tzedakah as an obligation directly connected to the privilege of ownership. Every single Jewish holiday, every single Jewish life cycle event, has its own tzedakah opportunity. It is perhaps the definitional mitzvah, the one which sets the standard for all other Jewish practices. We know that Jews are a giving people. Recent studies suggest that the vast majority of adult Jews make contributions to philanthropic causes. Yet, ironically, these righteous applications of their checkbooks and credit cards are often performed in secret. The more a family's commitment to tzedakah is shown to a child, the more it will become part of his or her life. Rosh Ha-Shanah is a wonderful time to start or renew this pattern.

Yom Kippur

Origins

Put yourself back into the time of the ancient Temple. Then, Yom Kippur offered some of the year's best spectacles. This was "old-time religion" at its best... Seven days before Yom Kippur, the High Priest moves from his home into a chamber in the Temple, devoting himself fully to God's service. This is the one time of the year that the High Priest has a direct involvement with the work of the sacrifices. On the eve of Yom Kippur, the High Priest pulls an all-nighter. Rather than sleeping, the night is spent in study and preparation. At the center of the day's ritual is a very special sacrifice. Two goats are brought before the High Priest. They are both perfect and equal animals. He draws lots from an urn. One goat becomes the sacrifice to be offered to God; the other will become the scapegoat. God's goat is sacrificed as a normative sin-offering. The other goat has a red string tied between its horns. Then the Torah tells us that the priest "shall lay both his hands on the head of the live goat and confess over it all the iniquities and transgressions of the Israelites, whatever the sin, putting them on the head of the goat. Then it shall be sent off into the wilderness...the goat shall carry all their sins."(Leviticus 16) In those days, worship was well-staged pageantry.

The climax, however, comes at the end of the day, just before a ceremony called *Neilah*, the closing of the gates. In the very heart of the Temple is a room called the Holy of Holies. Here is where the ark of the covenant, the original Torah Scroll, and the original tablets of the Ten Commandments are kept. Here is the one spot on earth where a person could most easily come close to God. The Holy of Holies is only entered once a year by one person. To end Yom Kippur, the High Priest goes into the Holy of Holies. It

---

> "...we are not denying the physical appetites their just place in life; we are simply recognizing the need of putting them in their place."

---

is a time of fear and trembling. Coming that close to God is the ultimate awesome experience. The entire nation holds its breath and waits. The High Priest asks God to forgive all the people's sins.

When the Temple was destroyed, the nature of Yom Kippur changed dramatically. Originally, Yom Kippur was a priests' holiday. Unlike other major Jewish celebrations, Yom Kippur had nothing to do with the agricultural cycle and was not the commemoration of a major historical event. Rather, it was a time for purifying the Temple (and those who worked there) just before Sukkot, the major celebration in the Jewish year. When the Temple was destroyed, the rabbis reworked the nature of the day. They centered it on prayer instead of pageantry. In an early midrash we hear this conversation, "Now that we have no prophet or High Priest or sacrifice, who shall atone for us? The only thing left to us

is prayer." (Tanchuma, Vayishlakh 10) This is a direct expression of something the prophet Hosea had taught earlier, "Instead of bullocks we will pay with the offerings of our lips." (14.3)

Three Opportunities

The celebration of Yom Kippur revolves around three mitzvot: resting, praying and afflicting the soul.

You shall afflict your soul: While extended and elaborate prayers fill the Day of Atonement, every school child knows that Yom Kippur is a day when you fast. Fasting is but one expression of the mitzvah,

"The tenth day of this seventh month shall be a Day of Atonement, it shall be a holy day of gathering, and you shall afflict your soul." (Lev. 23:26-27)

When the rabbis of the Talmud tried to define "afflicting the soul," they included abstaining from eating, wearing leather (a sign of wealth), washing, and sexual relations. This process of self-affliction was not conceived of as torture or mutilation,but rather as a dynamic statement of focus. Mordechai Kaplan explained it this way, "When we refrain from indulging our physical appetites for a limited period, in order to devote ourselves for a time more exclusively to demands that rank higher in our hierarchy of values, we are not denying the physical appetites their just place in life; we are simply recognizing the need of putting them in their place." (*The Meaning of God*, p. 169)

The mitzvah of fasting is one which applies to adult Jews—girls who are 12 years old or older, boys who are 13 or older. The Shulhan Arukh, the authoritative code of traditional Jewish law suggests that children under 9 not be allowed to fast (for reasons of health) and that children who are more than 9 should be trained gradually, starting with partial fasts and adding an hour a year as they grow. (O.H. 616.2) Fasting is also prohibited for anyone whose health might be at risk. The law code goes as far as stating, "Even if the patient claims that he can fast in spite of his illness, the advice of his physician should be followed." (O.H. 618.2) Special guidelines are also provided for pregnant mothers, encouraging them to eat as necessary. (O.H. 617.2ff)

Most parents are faced (in seemingly alternate years) with either encouraging or restricting their child's desires to fast. Many families have great success with skipping a meal, or limiting the kind of food eaten to the most simple and basic. In reality, almost any kind of trial fast will allow children to begin the process. The awareness, however, that parents take Yom Kippur seriously enough to fast (especially when serving food to a child) also makes a great impact. The bottom line, on fasting and the other traditional prohibitions, is the awareness that one day a year, the day given to self-evaluation, is taken very seriously. On Yom Kippur, we use a small act of self-discipline to encapsulate the most challenging of all self-disciplinary acts, true growth.

It shall be to you a Shabbat of solemn rest: Yom Kippur is also known as "the Sabbath of Sabbaths." All of the prohibitions about labor which apply to an ordinary Shabbat also apply to Yom Kippur, even more than they do on Rosh Ha-Shanah, where the command to refrain from working is not as intense. The creation of total rest was designed to create a day of community. On Yom Kippur the absence from work also adds to the totality of the day's self-directed focus. All distractions are taken away. The Torah teaches, "You shall do no work on that day, for it is a day of atonement, to make your atonement before the Lord your God." (Lev. 23:28)

You shall offer an offering of fire: Unlike Rosh Ha-Shanah, which had no special sacrifices, Yom Kippur was a day filled with special rituals. After the destruction of the Temple, these special rituals became transformed into the liturgy of the Synagogue. It is in the *Mahzor*, the High Holiday prayer book, and not in any outside rituals, that you will find the essence of this day.

If one were writing a guide book to the High Holidays, one of the "sights" a person should be advised not to miss is the *Neilah* service, the closing service which happens around sundown. It is the climax to the day. It is a short dramatic final burst of energy (like the last mile in a marathon). It ends with communal shouting, the blowing of the shofar, and a wonderful sense of joy and accomplishment. It is a moment to which children should be exposed. It is the "victory celebration" which climaxes the efforts of a very long 25-hour day.

FOOTNOTES

1. **Awe** is a feeling which overwhelms. It is a contradictory combination of fear and interest, excitement, respect, admiration and uncertainty. ירא /Awe doesn't translate or explain well. By definition, an awesome experience is one which is hard to talk about. The Hebrew root ירא (which means "awe") is sometimes translated as "fear" (e.g. God-fearing). Fear, however, is not the real meaning. It has more to do with "trembling". An awesome experience is one which causes us to "tremble." All "awe" does not originate in fearsomeness, but can be rooted in majesty, beauty, grace, scale.

   In talking about "awe" with children, it is *not* important to provide an exact definition. Rather, it is helpful to use experiences to clarify the feeling. Talk about seeing a sunset, counting all the stars until you can't count that high, seeing a famous movie star, etc. What *is* important, is to share the insight that some feelings are very powerful.

2. **Days of Awe.** Rosh Ha-Shanah comes on the first day of the Hebrew month of *Tishre*. Yom Kippur comes on the tenth day of that month. The first ten days of that month, including both holidays, are called the *aseret yemei t'shuvah*, the 10 days of repentance. The period of time from the first day of the Hebrew month of *Elul* (a month before Rosh Ha-Shanah) through the celebration of Sukkot (a holiday which begins in the middle of the month of *Tishre*) is called **The Days of Awe**.

   Special customs and practices set these days apart from the rest of the Jewish year. Starting on the first of *Elul*, the shofar is sounded every morning and a special set of prayers of atonement called *slihot* (forgiveness) are said daily. On the last Saturday night in *Elul*, the last Saturday night before Rosh Ha-Shanah, a special midnight *slihot* service is held.

   To explain the rhythm and tone of the High Holidays, the rabbis use the metaphor of a trial. In the midrash we are told, that on the first of *Elul*, the angels begin gathering evidence about the behavior of each Jew. On the last Saturday night of the month, at midnight, this evidence is brought before the heavenly court. That night indictments are handed down. On Rosh Ha-Shanah, the trial is held. On Yom Kippur, the heavenly court will pass judgment. The in-between days are the time to ask for mercy, these are the "Days of Repentance." Tradition holds that God will wait to record the verdict all the way up until the *Shemini Atzeret*, the last day of Sukkot.

   The rituals and metaphors of this period are designed to evoke a sense of awe. They capitalize on the anxiety of being judged to compel Jews into a process of self-evaluation and reflection which will help them to maximize the potential of the next year. These "Days of Awe" have an aspect of trembling, both of fear and of expectation.

3. **Hallah** is a special "ritual" bread which is eaten at Shabbat dinners and on holidays. Bread is the "essential" food, and the process of eating Jewishly centers on the eating of bread. The blessing said over the eating of bread is the ritual act which makes the act of eating an encounter with the sacred. Likewise, the *birkat hamazon*, the grace said after eating, is really the blessing said after eating bread. The Hallah we make and eat is a remembrance of the Hallot (plural) brought to the Temple as part of the tithing of grain which was grown.

   The Judaism we know emerged from the farm. The Torah carefully regulated farmers. Jews were never allowed to imagine that they fully owned the land or anything it produced. Always, there were tithes. Portions of everything raised and everything grown had to be shared. Part of it was a gift-offering, an acknowledgment that without God's help, nothing would have grown. Part of it went to the Temple, an expression of a national unity of purpose. Part of it was left for the widow, the poor, the orphan and the stranger. Ownership brought the responsibility to share that which God allowed us to produce with those in need. For biblical farmers, hallah had nothing to do with Shabbat or holidays. It was something taken every time dough was made, the fulfillment of the commandment found in Numbers 15.19-20.

   The round Hallah used on Rosh Ha-Shanah is a folk tradition. Its purpose is unclear. There are many explanations: A crown which reminds us of God's Rulership, the endless cycle of the seasons, a way to make the day stand out as special.

4. **The Birthday of the Universe.** Rosh Ha-Shanah, the Jewish New Year, is sometimes called "The birthday of the universe." In one of the holiday's most significant pieces of liturgy, *ha-yom ha-rat olam*, we are told "Today the universe was created." It is a simple, joyful image, which stands in marked contrast to the awesome nature of most of the day's images. It is for this reason that many children's treatments of the holiday center on a universal birthday cake (along with apples and honey).

   Ironically, the actual prayer from which the image is drawn, establishes "creation day" as a day of judgment, and is one of the most somber pieces in the service. In actuality, the midrashic tradition saw Rosh Ha-Shanah as the anniversary of the sixth day of creation, not the first. It was on Friday of the first week, the sixth day, that Adam and Eve broke God's command,

44

were punished, repented and reestablished their relation with their Creator. The Jewish New Year was set on the anniversary of those events, a model for the process of repentance and reconciliation.

While the birthday party image is an easily accessible one, and one useful for explaining the special nature of a very abstract holiday to young children, it is important to remember that a real understanding of these holidays rests in understanding the cycle of repentance and renewal.

5. **The Shofar** is an announcing tool made from a ram's horn. Hearing it sound (100 times) is the essential *mitzvah* of Rosh Ha-Shanah.

On the second day of Rosh Ha-Shanah, we read the story of the Binding of Isaac (Genesis 22). The story concludes with a ram replacing Isaac as the gift-offering. The midrash teaches that every time God hears the call of the shofar, God is reminded of the promises made to Abraham to protect his future-family. Other Jewish sources interpret the call of the shofar as a call to "awaken" and as a call to be aware of "danger."

6. **Tekiah, Shevarim, Teru'ah.** The sounding of the shofar is done through a combination of four basic patterns. *Tekiah*, a long loud blast, sounded like a shout. *Shevarim*, three short blasts, sounded like a groan. *Teru'ah*, nine quick blasts sounded like crying. In addition, the *Tekiah Gedolah*, an extended *Tekiah*, is used to conclude the sounding.

The rabbis learn from the Torah that the sounding of the Shofar should consist of a combination of two basic sounds. Different biblical verses (Numbers 29.1 and Numbers 10.5) use the verbs *tekiah*, and *teru'ah* to describe the mitzvah of sounding and hearing the shofar. Normally, the sounding of the shofar would have consisted of only these two sounds plus the extended *tekiah* (which is extrapolated from Psalms 81.4). However, the Talmud tells of a conversation which took place in the third century. There is an argument over the kind of sound the intended by the verb *teru'ah*. Some thought that it meant the present sounding, others thought it should be sounded like the present *shevarim*. Rabbi Abbahu worked out a compromise, introducing the *shevarim* (which means broken) as a third sound in the formula. (Rosh Ha-Shanah 34a).

Like many Jewish ritual actions, the procedure for sounding the shofar has been clearly defined, but the meaning has not. Specific rules regulate the kind of shofar which may be used, the order of the sounding, the time and places where it may be done. Each of us is left to find our own understandings of its call. Perhaps, it is in that context that Saul Lieberman called it "a prayer without words."

7. **Maimonides** was a 12th and 13th century Jewish scholar who wrote one of the most important codes of Jewish law, the *Mishneh Torah*. In the passage quoted, he describes the sounds of the shofar as a call for spiritual awakening.

8. **Isaac ben Moses Arama** was a 15th century Spanish Jewish scholar who moved to Italy after the expulsion of the Jews from Spain. His major works, a book of philosophy, was called *Akedat Yitzhak*, the "Binding of Isaac." Arama is often known as the *Akedat Yitzhak*. Many Jewish scholars are known by the names of their major work. In his comment on the sounds of the shofar, Arama talks about the emotions evoked by the different calls.

9. **Mahzor** is the name of the special prayer book used on the High Holidays. Its name

evolves from the Hebrew word for "repetition" and means "a cycle." This is similar to the image evoked by the word *Siddur*, the name of the daily prayerbook, which means "order." In both cases, the names reflect an understanding that the liturgy is part of the person praying, not something to be read. In each case, the book served as a reminder of the order and form of the blessings.

10. **Atonement.** The word atonement really does come from the words AT and ONE, probably derived from the archaic "one-ment" which meant agreement. The lesson to be learned from this etymology (apologies to Eric Segal) is that atonement isn't saying you're sorry, it is reestablishing the relationship.

11. **Miss the Mark.** In the Torah, Aaron is told how to deal with "the iniquities (*avonot*) of the children of Israel, all their transgressions (*pesha'im*) and all their sins (*hataim*)." When the rabbis read this verse, (Yoma 36b) they felt a need to understand the difference between an *avon*, a *pesha*, and a *heyt*. They came to an understanding that a *heyt* (a sin) was an accidental act, an *avon* was an act of self-aware wrong-doing, and a *pesha* was an act of full rebellion. It was possible to make atonement for each of these levels of misbehavior. No matter how great the violation, it was always possible to return.

It was to this end that the image of "missing the mark" was evolved. Sin was seen as behavior which fell short of a person's potential. In the book of Ecclesiastes (7.20) we are told, "There is not one perfect man on earth who always does what is best and does not err." It is this understanding of human behavior which makes Yom Kippur a necessary event. While understanding human weakness, it also allows for the full maximization of human potential. In this context, Philo, a famous Jewish philosopher, wrote, "Sin, if repented, is not a stain on a person, for absolute sinlessness belongs only to God alone...the grace which God gives to one who repents is the same as that which is given to one who is entirely innocent."

While a sin is indeed an act of wrongdoing, a tendency towards evil, it is not definitionally the essence of a person. The potential for becoming better always exists. It is to that end that the tradition thinks in terms of "missing the mark," and returning to do better.

12. **T'shuvah** is the Hebrew word for repentance. It comes from a root which means "return." In Judaism, return is the essence of repentance. In the book of Hosea, we are given a prime example. Hosea the prophet is married to a "working-woman." She cheats on him. The relationship is broken over and over again. The gap between the two of them is great. God then orders Hosea to restore the relationship, to seek a reconciliation. The two of them unite, and believable commitments are made never to again violate the trust and obligation of their vows. This life experience is a metaphor for the relationship between God and Israel. A vow of mutual commitment is cheated upon and shattered. Yet it can be restored. This is the embodiment of the lesson taught by the prophet Zechariah (1.3) "Return to Me—says the Lord of Hosts—and I will return to you." This is t'shuvah.

FOR THE TEACHER

This High Holiday volume of **Building Jewish Life** centers on these goals:

Days of Awe

1. To introduce the feeling of "awe" as a combination of fear and excitement.
2. To expose students to several key pieces of High Holiday Liturgy including *Avinu Malkeinu*, *Kol Nidre*, and *Al Heyt*.

Rosh Ha-Shanah

1. To explain that, like the first day of school, Rosh Ha-Shanah is a "new beginning."
2. To present the four calls made by the shofar and invite students to explore their message.

Yom Kippur

1. To explain that ATONEMENT means returning to be AT ONE with yourself and with God.
2. To use the image of a bow and arrow to explain that *t'shuvah* means coming back from having missed the mark.

ESSENTIAL VOCABULARY

Rosh Ha-Shanah

awe	A combination of fear and excitement
Rosh Ha-Shanah	The Jewish New Year, lit., "Head of the Year"
L'shanah Tovah	Happy New Year
shofar	A musical instrument made from a ram's horn
Tekiah, Teru'ah, Shevarim	The names of the shofar calls
Mahzor	The High Holiday Prayer book

Yom Kippur

atonement	Making amends. Returning to be "at one"
Shabbat ha-Shabbaton	The Sabbath of Sabbaths, another name for Yom Kippur
missing the mark	A translation of the Hebrew word "het," usually understood as "sin"
T'shuvah	Returning from "missing the mark" to doing the right thing. Hebrew for repentance

Liturgy

Kol Nidre	A special Yom Kippur prayer which reminds us to be careful about our words and our promises
Al Het	A prayer which lists different ways people miss the mark
Avinu Malkeinu	A prayer which asks God to forgive us, because God is like our Parent and our Ruler

ADDITIONAL VOCABULARY

musical instrument	like a guitar or piano
shrieking	shouting
hollow	something empty on the inside
ancient	something from a long time ago
slumber	another word for sleep
curse	words which wish someone bad luck
worship	praying to God
notice	to see
image	a shape or form
captives	prisoners
ruler	like a king or queen
expresses	says
justice	doing what is right
weapons	things used in war
subjects	people who live in a country ruled by a king or queen
archery	the sport of shooting with a bow and arrow
fasting	not eating on purpose
authority	the power to make others obey
Bet Din	a Jewish court
Yeshiva	a Jewish school

We know that the schedule of classes around the High Holiday period is often chaotic and uneven. It is impossible to predict or prescribe the number of sessions which will be possible prior to the actual celebration of the holidays. While we will include material for four lessons, we fully expect that most teachers will find time for only one or two lessons.

It should also be pointed out that the best time to teach about the High Holidays is not the fall but the spring. It can effectively be taught as the last unit of the year, as a preparation for the following fall.

Teachers should feel free to adapt and improvise according to (1) time available, (2) age and ability of students, (3) involvement of families, (4) previous background, and (5) moments of inspiration.

LESSON ONE

Rosh Ha-Shanah: New Beginnings

1. **SET INDUCTION:** ASK each of your students to share one thing they think of about the first day of school. TALK about the feelings a student feels when thinking about going into a new class with a new teacher. INTRODUCE the word "awe" as the combination of fear and excitement.

2. **READING ABOUT ROSH HA-SHANAH:** READ pages 3 through 8 together. STOP to point out each time one of the things suggested by the students appears in the text. ASK students to redefine the word "awe" in their own words. ASK them to explain how Rosh Ha-Shanah is like the first day of school.

3. **THE JEWISH CALENDAR:** TURN to page 76. EXPLAIN that the Jewish calendar is different from the one used in America. IDENTIFY the calendar as showing the month of September. (You may want to point out that this is not this year's calendar). INTRODUCE the months of *Elul* and *Tishre*

holidays of Rosh Ha-Shanah, Yom Kippur and Sukkot. POINT OUT *Slihot*, the midnight "forgive me" service held on the last Saturday night before Rosh Ha-Shanah, and *Shabbat Shuvah*, the special Shabbat between Rosh Ha-Shanah and Yom Kippur. ASSIGN page 30, Preparing for Rosh Ha-Shanah, as homework to be done with parents.

4. **MAKING ROSH HA-SHANAH CARDS:** INTRODUCE the phrase *"L'shanah Tovah,"* have a happy New Year. USE the art medium of your preference. HAVE every student make a card. Where necessary, help students WRITE DOWN their wishes for the coming year. Here is an activity where aides will be of great assistance. Each student should get special attention.

5. **APPLES & HONEY:** END the day with a special snack of Apples and Honey, or a Round Hallah and Honey. WISH everyone a *"L'shanah Tovah."*

LESSON TWO
Rosh Ha-Shanah: The Shofar

1. **SET INDUCTION:** BRING a shofar into class. INTRODUCE the object. PASS it around, let everyone try to make a sound from it. DISCUSS the origins of the shofar.

2. **READING ABOUT THE SHOFAR:** READ pages 9 through 15 together. HAVE students EXPLAIN what both Maimonides and Isaac Arama heard in the shofar calls.

3. **HEARING THE SHOFAR CALLS:** LET the students HEAR the four different calls made by the shofar. If you can't blow the shofar yourself, then invite the rabbi, educator or a local shofar blower into class to help you. Otherwise, arrange to have a tape of the calls.

ASK students to try to SOUND each of the calls on the shofar. ALSO, Have the class sing the right sound for each of the calls. PRACTICE them.

4. **PRACTICE THE SHOFROT:** (OPTIONAL) READ the story "The Announcing Tool" from *BJL Rosh Ha-Shanah Mahzor* (pages 22-27). You may want to act it out.

(OPTIONAL) Then read together the Shofrot service from *BJL Rosh Ha-Shanah Mahzor*, pages 28-29. HAVE students sing the shofar sounds, or have the shofar blown.

TURN to page 31. Have students REVIEW the shofar calls by completing the exercise. ASSIGN the story on page 32 as HOMEWORK for students to do with their parents.

5. **REVIEW:** GO OVER the things they have learned about the shofar. MAKE a list of everything they can remember on the blackboard. SING the shofar calls one more time. WISH everyone *"L'shanah Tovah."*

LESSON THREE
Yom Kippur: T'shuvah

1. **SET INDUCTION:** BRING three bean bags to class. PLACE the wastebasket on the far side of the room. EXPLAIN to students that anyone who can't toss all three bean bags into the wastebasket will be out. MAKE SURE that most students will not be able to toss all three bean bags into the basket. OFFER a practice round. After the practice round, ASK: "How many students think they can stay in this game?" Most hands should **not** be raised. *If most of the class believes they can get all three in, make it harder and then ask again.* ASK: "Why can't you all get all three in?" ANSWER: "It is too hard." ASK: "If I let you take back any bean bags which miss, and let you try again, how many of you think you can make it?"

EXPLAIN that Yom Kippur is a day when you get to take back mistakes and try again. INTRODUCE two ideas. (1) That when you do something wrong, you are *missing the mark*. You are not being the best person you could be. (2) *T'shuvah* is the way we "take back" things which have *missed the mark* and try again.

2. **READING ABOUT YOM KIPPUR:** WRITE the word ATONEMENT on the black board. EXPLAIN that Yom Kippur, the holiest day in the Jewish year, is called the Day of Atonement. ASK: "Who can find two words hidden in the word atonement." ESTABLISH the words AT and ONE. EXPLAIN, that Yom Kippur is when we return (do *t'shuvah*) from *missing the mark* and again become "AT ONE" with God.

TURN to page 18. READ through the section on Yom Kippur with the class. STOP to point out and REVIEW each of the major concepts: being AT ONE, *missing the mark*, and *t'shuvah*. MAKE SURE that students can EXPLAIN each of these ideas in their own words.

3. PRACTICING T'SHUVAH: TURN to page 33. READ the directions together. MAKE sure that students understand how to fill in this exercise. Also TELL them that all of their answers will be a secret. Have them COMPLETE the exercise. If NECESSARY, read the exercise out loud, and have them circle the answers they choose. When they are done, have them CLOSE their books and NOT SHOW them to anyone.

ASK: "What did you learn from this exercise? Were you surprised by any of your answers? Are you better in some things than others? Do you know the areas where you will have to work hard this year? ALLOW an open discussion.

ASK: "Was filling out this chart an act of *t'shuvah?*" ANSWER: "No." This is only the first part of *t'shuvah*. The first step is knowing the things which you have done. The rest of the job is to direct your heart so that you will never ever *miss the mark* in the same way again.

4. ROLE PLAYING T'SHUVAH (Part II) TURN to page 25. READ for the second time about the two ways that people can *miss the mark*. REVIEW the difference between things which "hurt" God and things which "hurt" people. EXPLAIN that all things we do wrong *miss the mark* in God's eyes. If you do real *t'shuvah*, God will forgive all mistakes. But, God won't forgive anything which *missed the mark* by hurting another person, until that person has forgiven you. CONCLUDE: In order to make *t'shuvah* on Yom Kippur, you must first make up things with all the people you deal with over the year. This means saying, "I'm sorry."

EXPLAIN: It is not always easy to admit that you have done something wrong, and then say "I'm sorry." We are going to practice doing *t'shuvah* by acting out some situations where people say "I am sorry." MOVE the class into a circle. PICK students to act out these situations:

A. A student cheats on a test. The teacher doesn't catch him/her. He gets an A in the course. Just before Yom Kippur, the student comes to the teacher s/he had last year and says "I am sorry."

B. A teacher makes a mistake in grading an important test. The student who should have gotten an A got a C. Later, the teacher discovers the mistake. It is too late to change the grade. S/he has to tell the student, "I am sorry."

C. A younger child borrows his/her brother/sister's Walkman without asking and breaks the headphones. S/he has to tell the truth and say, "I am sorry."

D. A parent has a bad day at work. When s/he comes home, the kids are being loud, not bad. The parent yells at them and punishes them. Later, s/he realizes the mistake. S/he must say, "I am sorry."

E. A child asks his/her parents to buy an expensive toy. They say no. The child yells and screams and calls them the worst parents in the world. Later, s/he is sorry. Now, s/he must say, "I am sorry."

MAKE UP other situations. TALK about why it is hard to say "I am sorry."

5. CLOSURE: REVIEW the things you have done. HAVE the students define: ATONEMENT, *missing the mark*, and *t'shuvah*. To

CONCLUDE: READ or TELL them the story found on pages 4-6 of the *BJL Yom Kippur Mahzor* (OPTIONAL). ASSIGN students to read the story of Elana (pages 34-38) with their parents and complete the exercise.

LESSON FOUR
Yom Kippur: Special Prayers
Material can be found in BJL Yom Kipput Mahzor

1. SET INDUCTION: ASK students to describe their memories of Rosh Ha-Shanah services. Have them SHARE the things they remember seeing, hearing, doing or feeling. Feelings will be the hardest. You may need to redirect this part of the task. Make a LIST of these things on the black-board.

Prepare to PLAY a recording of the *Kol Nidre* (or better, bring someone into class who can sing the *Kol Nidre*.) INTRODUCE the *Kol Nidre* as a very important prayer which is said at the evening service which begins Yom Kippur. DIRECT the class to listen to the prayer and see if they can find its feeling. You may want to provide paper and crayons for them to "draw the feeling." PLAY the tape and talk about how it feels.

2. STUDYING THE KOL NIDRE: EXPLAIN that the *Kol Nidre* is a prayer which talks about words. TURN to page 2. READ or tell the story found here. ASK: "Why do we have to be very careful about the way we use words?" ESTABLISH that words can hurt people, and that words are very hard to take back.

TURN to page 7. READ the second half of the *Kol Nidre*. (May we keep all the promises we make...). ASK students to EXPLAIN what this prayer means in their own words. COMPARE the "meaning" of the *Kol Nidre* with the "feeling" of the *Kol Nidre*.

3. EXPRESSING THESE PRAYERS: BREAK the class into four groups. ASSIGN each group one of these four special prayers.

Avinu Malkeinu	page 23	
Shofrot	page 28-29	*BJL Rosh Ha-Shanah Mahzor*
Kol Nidre	page 7	
Al Heyt	page 21	

DIRECT each group to DESIGN and DRAW a mural which explains their prayer. HELP them begin by asking them to pick one sentence from their prayer. WRITE it on the top of the mural paper. PROVIDE them with appropriate art supplies. It would be best to insure each group's success by providing them with a teacher aide or a volunteer parent.

4. CLOSURE: REVIEW the four prayers you have looked at. If you have time, the best way to end this lesson would be to PRACTICE all (or some) of the Yom Kippur service.